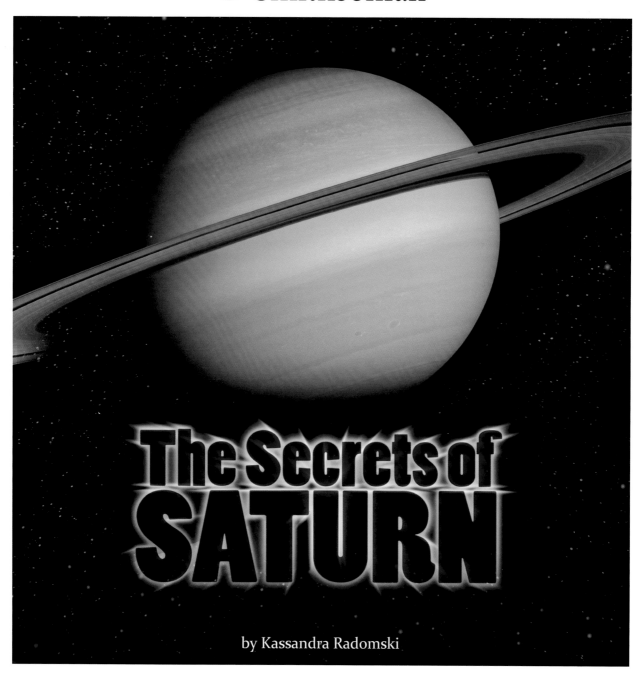

Smithsonian

The Secrets of SATURN

by Kassandra Radomski

CAPSTONE PRESS
a capstone imprint

Capstone Press
1710 Roe Crest Drive, North Mankato, Minnesota 56003
www.capstonepub.com

Library of Congress Cataloging-in-Publication Data
Radomski, Kassandra, author.
  The secrets of Saturn / by Kassandra Radomski.
    pages cm. — (Smithsonian. Planets)
  Summary: "Discusses the planet Saturn, including observations by ancient cultures, current knowledge of Saturn, and plans for future scientific research and space exploration"—Provided by publisher.
  Audience: Ages 8–10
  Audience: Grades 2 to 4
  ISBN 978-1-4914-5868-6 (library binding)
  ISBN 978-1-4914-5901-0 (paperback)
  ISBN 978-1-4914-5912-6 (eBook PDF)
1. Saturn (Planet)—Juvenile literature. 2. Saturn (Planet)—Exploration—Juvenile literature. I. Title.
  QB671.R33 2016
  523.46—dc23   2014046198

Editorial Credits
Elizabeth R. Johnson, editor; Tracy Davies McCabe and Kazuko Collins, designers;
Wanda Winch, media researcher; Tori Abraham, production specialist

Our very special thanks to Andrew K. Johnston, Geographer, Center for Earth and Planetary Studies, National Air and Space Museum, Smithsonian Institution, for his curatorial review. Capstone would also like to thank Kealy Gordon, Smithsonian Institution Product Development Manager, and the following at Smithsonian Enterprises: Ellen Nanney, Licensing Manager; Brigid Ferraro, Director of Licensing; Carol LeBlanc, Senior Vice President, Consumer & Education Products; Chris Liedel, President.

Photo Credits
Black Cat Studios: Ron Miller, 13 (top), 23; © Calvin J. Hamilton, 11; Courtesy of Carolyn Porco, Cassini Imaging Team Leader, Director CICLOPS/photo by Phil Mumford, 36; Getty Images: UIG/Encyclopaedia Britannica, 17 (bottom), Universal Images Group, 9 (bottom); Granger, NYC, 9 (t); Library of Congress: Prints and Photographs Division, 8 (right); Lunar and Planetary Institute, 5 (bottom); NASA: Ames Research Center, 18 (t), ESA/Hubble Heritage Team (StScI/AURA)/M.H. Wong (StScI/UC Berkeley) and C.Go (Philippines), 20, JPL, 5 (back), 19 (all), 22, 29, JPL/ESA/ISS/Cassini Imaging Team, 13 (b), JPL/Space Science Institute, cover, back cover, 1, 18 (b), 24, JPL-Caltech, 25, JPL-Caltech/SSI, 14, 15, JPL-Caltech/University of Arizona/University of Idaho, 21; Rijksmuseum, Amsterdam, 7; Robert Kelly: Canon XS through an 8-inch reflector telescope, 6; Science Source/Lionel Bret, 17 (t), Royal Astronomical Society, 8 (left); Shutterstock: OHishiapply, space background

Direct Quotations
Page 27 from the October 2007 TED Talk, "This is Saturn," www.ted.com

Printed in Canada.
032015   008825FRF15

Table of Contents

Secretive Saturn................................. 4

Ancient Beliefs 6

A Planet with "Handles" 8

The Gas Giant................................... 10

Weather Far from the Sun 12

Mysterious Weather Patterns 14

Stunning Rings................................. 16

First Missions to Saturn 18

Exploring the Dark Moon Titan 20

Exploring the Bright Moon Enceladus 24

Seeking Answers 26

What Will Scientists Find Next? 28

Glossary 30

Read More...................................... 31

Internet Sites................................. 31

Critical Thinking Using the Common Core........ 32

Index 32

Secretive Saturn

Saturn may be the most easily recognized planet in our solar system. Images of this golden planet with its massive collection of rings are breathtaking. Saturn is classified as a gas giant planet. It is the second largest planet in the solar system.

Photographs have helped scientists learn a lot about Saturn, including its collection of rings and moons. The Cassini spacecraft has been studying Saturn for more than 10 years. It has helped unlock many of Saturn's secrets. However, there are still many unanswered questions and mysteries.

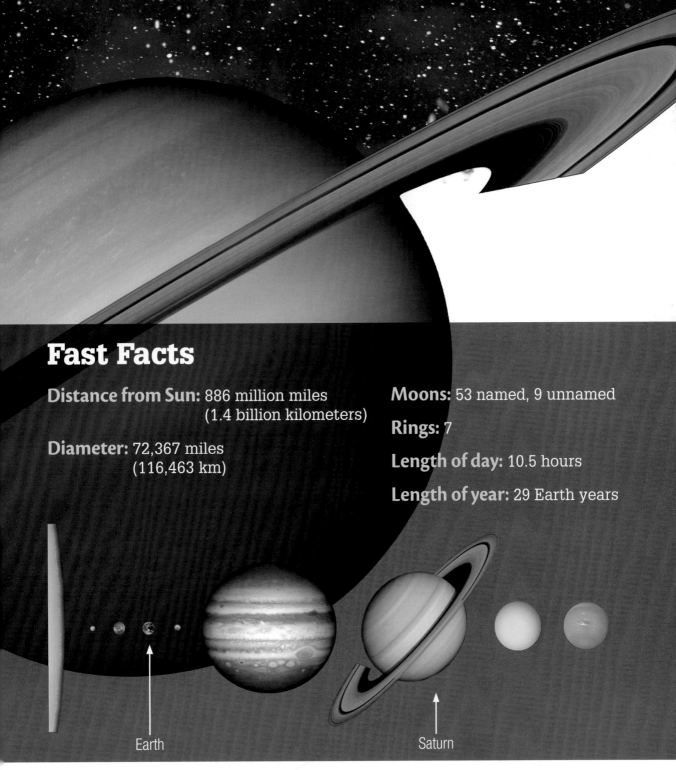

Fast Facts

Distance from Sun: 886 million miles
(1.4 billion kilometers)

Diameter: 72,367 miles
(116,463 km)

Moons: 53 named, 9 unnamed

Rings: 7

Length of day: 10.5 hours

Length of year: 29 Earth years

Earth

Saturn

Ancient Beliefs

Because Saturn is one of the planets that can be seen without a telescope, people have known about it for thousands of years. In 700 BC the Assyrians described Saturn as a "sparkle in the night." The ancient Greeks thought Saturn was a wandering star. They named it after Kronus, the Greek god of agriculture. The name we use today comes from Saturnus, the Roman god of agriculture. Saturnus was also Jupiter's father.

Spying Saturn in the Night Sky

Ancient cultures could only see Saturn as a point of light. But today we can see the planets in more detail with just a small telescope or a pair of binoculars. Find Saturn in the night sky and you may even be able to see the shape of its rings!

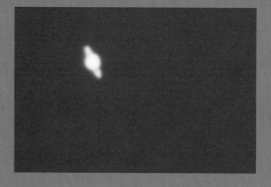

Assyria was located in parts of modern-day Iraq, Syria, and Turkey.

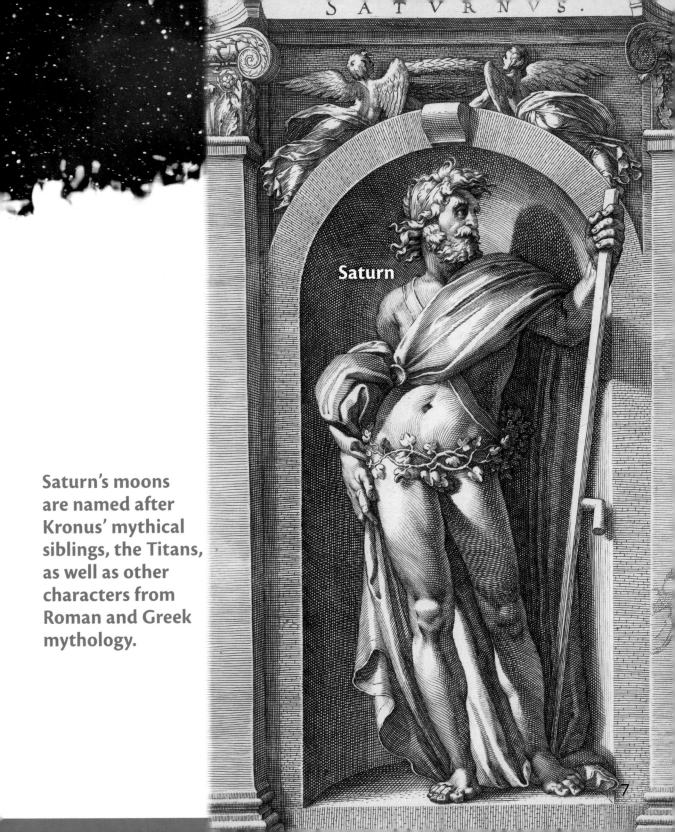

Saturn

Saturn's moons are named after Kronus' mythical siblings, the Titans, as well as other characters from Roman and Greek mythology.

A Planet with "Handles"

Italian astronomer Galileo Galilei was the first person to look at Saturn through a telescope in 1610. To him it looked like Saturn was made up of three connected planets. He drew sketches of Saturn that made it look like a cup with handles on each side. He didn't know that planets could have rings, because no one had ever seen them before.

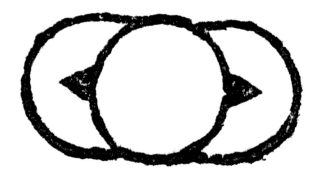

Dutch astronomer Christian Huygens looked at Saturn through a more powerful telescope in 1659. He believed the handles Galileo drew were actually one thin, flat ring that went around Saturn. Huygens also discovered Saturn's largest moon, Titan.

French astronomer Jean-Dominique Cassini found four other moons between 1671 and 1684. Cassini was also the first to notice a gap that divides Saturn's rings into two parts. That gap is now called the Cassini Division.

Scientists did not know any other planets had rings until Uranus' rings were discovered through a telescope in 1977.

The Gas Giant

Saturn is called a gas giant because it is almost entirely made of gas. It has no solid surface. The surface you see in photographs is actually Saturn's cloudy atmosphere. The inner planets, Mercury, Venus, Earth, and Mars, have rock and metal below their clouds, but Saturn is mostly made up of hydrogen and helium gases. Saturn's powerful gravity pulls the gases into a spherical shape and keeps the gases from floating off into space.

Although Saturn is a gas giant, there are parts of the planet that are not gas. Moving inward from the gaseous atmosphere, there is a gradual change to a liquid interior. This may be a layer of melted ice. Beneath the liquid layer is Saturn's solid inner core, made of melted rock. Saturn's inner core is about the size of Earth.

Saturn's gases give the planet a low density. It has the lowest density of all the planets in our solar system. An object with the same density as Saturn would float in water.

Helium is often used inside balloons to make them float in the air.

Scientists use theories about how planets form to figure out the sizes of their cores.

Weather Far from the Sun

Saturn is a bitterly cold planet. The distance between the Sun and Saturn is 10 times longer than the distance between the Sun and Earth. Saturn's solid inner core provides more heat to the planet than the Sun does, but most of Saturn's heat escapes into space. The average temperature on Saturn is -288 degrees Fahrenheit (-178 °Celsius). That's much colder than Earth's average temperature of about 58 °F (14 °C).

Not only is Saturn colder than Earth, the wind on Saturn blows faster than any wind on Earth. At Saturn's equator, wind speeds reach up to 1,100 miles (1,770 km) per hour. The fastest winds on Earth occur during hurricanes and only reach about 246 miles (396 km) per hour.

artist illustration of Saturn's atmosphere

Saturn's Colors

Saturn gets its gold color from sunlight reflecting off its clouds. The yellow and gold bands in the planet's atmosphere are created by Saturn's super fast winds and its hot interior. The light stripes are called zones. The dark stripes are called belts. The zones and belts rotate around the planet in opposite directions.

Mysterious Weather Patterns

Like Earth, Saturn has storms with hurricane-like winds. The area surrounding the north pole has strong winds that have been spinning for at least 30 years. This weather pattern is unique because it stays inside a six-sided area that scientists call "the hexagon." This is different from Earth's hurricanes, which travel across the warm Pacific and Atlantic oceans and weaken once they hit land.

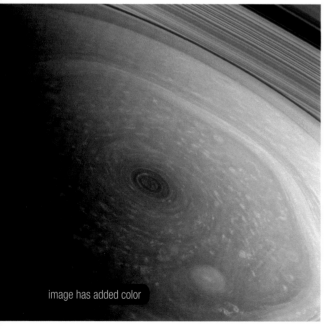

image has added color

Saturn also experiences occasional storms called Great White Spots. The largest observed storm occurred in 2010 and lasted for seven months. It started as a small white cloud. Over time it became a huge stormy band that circled the entire planet. After the storm, scientists discovered energy had been released into Saturn's atmosphere. They believe this energy caused Saturn's temperature to temporarily increase by 150 °F (66 °C).

Dec. 5, 2010

Jan. 2, 2011

Feb. 25, 2011

Apr. 22, 2011

May 18, 2011

Aug. 12, 2011

images from Saturn's largest observed storm

Stunning Rings

While Saturn is one of four planets in the solar system that has rings, Saturn's are the most impressive. The collection of rings orbits the equator and stretches about 175,000 miles (282,000 km) across. But the thickness of most of the rings may be only about 30 feet (9 meters).

Saturn's rings are made up of ice, rocks, and dust particles. Some of the pieces are as small as a grain of sugar, and others are as large as a house. The pieces of rock and ice may have fallen from comets, asteroids, or one of Saturn's moons. Gravity from Saturn and its moons keeps the rings in place.

If Earth had rings as wide as Saturn's, they would reach three-quarters of the way to the Moon.

artist illustration of rings

Naming the Rings

Saturn's rings were named alphabetically in the order they were discovered. Their distances from the planet have nothing to do with the letter names they were given. The gaps between the rings also have names.

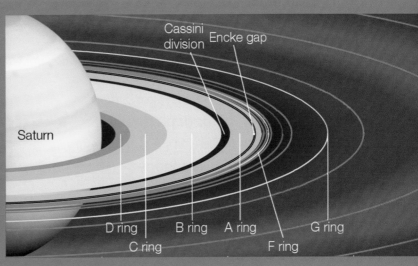

Cassini division

Encke gap

Saturn

D ring

C ring

B ring

A ring

F ring

G ring

The Cassini Division is a gap between the B and A rings. It measures 2,920 miles (4,699 km) across.

First Missions to Saturn

Pioneer 11

The first spacecraft to take close-up images of Saturn was Pioneer 11. It flew by Jupiter first and reached Saturn in September 1979. It discovered two of Saturn's moons and the F ring.

Voyagers

Voyager 1 and Voyager 2 flew by Saturn in 1980 and 1981, taking thousands of pictures of Saturn's rings and larger moons.

One image of Saturn's B ring showed finger-like shadows never seen before. They are now called "spokes." The spokes form in minutes and disappear within two hours. Scientists still don't know what causes them.

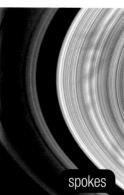

spokes

The Voyager missions provided new information and also raised many questions. Answers to those questions had to wait, because the next mission to Saturn wasn't until 1997.

Cassini-Huygens

The two-part Cassini-Huygens spacecraft launched in 1997. It took seven years to reach Saturn. Since Cassini's arrival in 2004, it has studied Saturn's rings, taken pictures of Saturn's huge storm in 2010, and explored Saturn's moons.

The Cassini-Huygens spacecraft is named for astronomers Christian Huygens and Jean-Dominique Cassini.

Exploring the Dark Moon Titan

So far astronomers have found 62 moons orbiting Saturn. Only 53 of them have been officially named. Titan is Saturn's largest moon. In 2005 the Cassini spacecraft released the Huygens probe over Titan. At the time Titan was the largest unexplored body in the solar system. With the help of a parachute, the probe landed safely on Titan's surface. Titan is dark, cold, and misty, with temperatures reaching as low as -289 °F (-178 °C).

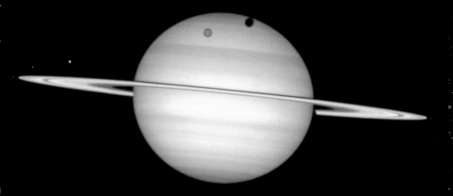

moons cross in front of Saturn

Secrets in the Sea

Images taken in 2013 and 2014 from the Cassini spacecraft show an object in Titan's largest sea. This object did not appear in photos taken earlier. It could be bubbles rising to the surface—or something else. It's still a secret!

Titan is large enough to be a planet—it's bigger than Mercury! It is classified as a moon because it orbits Saturn, not the Sun.

Images from the Huygens probe have helped scientists uncover a moon that has some things in common with Earth. Titan has a thick atmosphere like Earth. It has mountains, plains, sand dunes, and deserts like Earth. Titan also has eroded coastlines, and a string of lakes and seas near its north and south poles. The lakes and seas are made up of liquid ethane and methane instead of water. It even rains methane on Titan.

Like Earth, Titan undergoes seasonal changes. But instead of lasting a few months like the seasons on Earth, Titan's seasons last seven years.

Huygens Probe

It took 2 hours and 27 minutes for the Huygens probe to travel through Titan's atmosphere and reach the surface. Once it landed, the probe sent data for 72 minutes before its batteries died. More than 10 years later, scientists are still working through all the data.

Rainfall may only happen on Titan every 30 years or so, for 10 to 100 hours at a time.

artist illustration of Titan

Exploring the Bright Moon Enceladus

Enceladus is another one of Saturn's moons that is getting a lot of attention. Enceladus is a stunning bright white moon with cracks on its surface. Images from the Cassini spacecraft have helped scientists discover geysers of water shooting out from cracks in the moon's south pole.

When the geysers were first discovered, it was not clear what caused them to erupt. Researchers discovered an underground ocean of liquid water beneath the surface of Enceladus in 2014. That ocean could be the source of the geysers. The liquid water on Enceladus could even make it possible for small life forms to exist there.

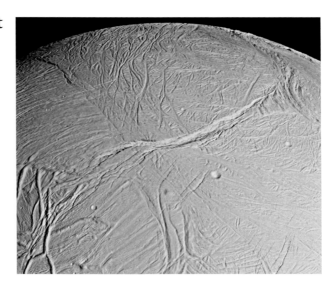

Enceladus = en-SELL-a-dus

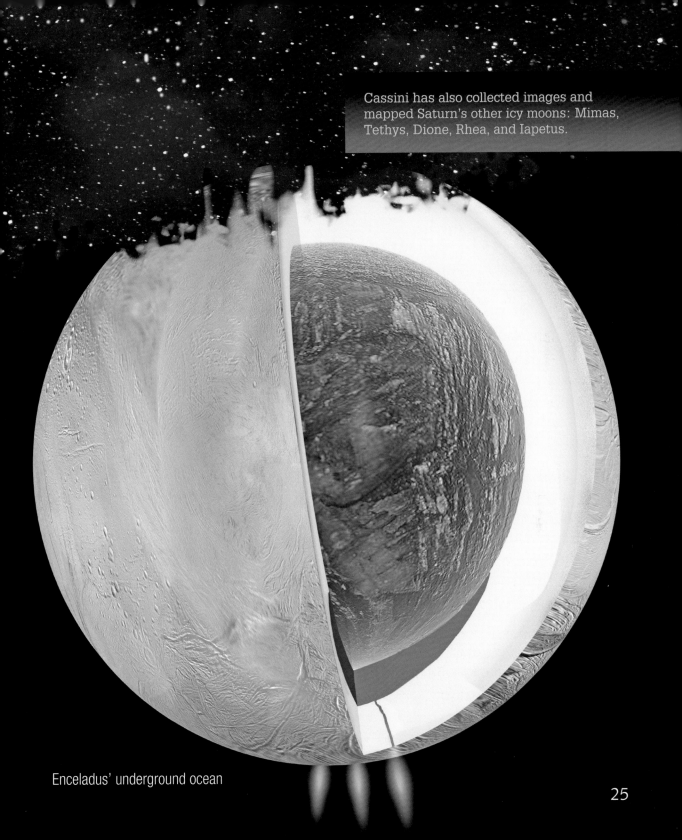

Cassini has also collected images and mapped Saturn's other icy moons: Mimas, Tethys, Dione, Rhea, and Iapetus.

Enceladus' underground ocean

Seeking Answers

Scientist Spotlight: Carolyn Porco

Carolyn Porco is a scientist who studies the planets. Her interest in astronomy started when she was a teenager growing up in New York. She remembers when she saw Saturn for the first time through her friend's telescope. When she was in college, Porco worked with a group that took pictures of Saturn, Jupiter, Uranus, and Neptune for the Voyager mission. Now she leads the team in charge of taking images of Saturn and its moons from the Cassini spacecraft. She has won numerous awards and honors over the years. In 2012 she was named one of *Time* magazine's 25 most influential people in space. She's even had an asteroid named after her: Porco.

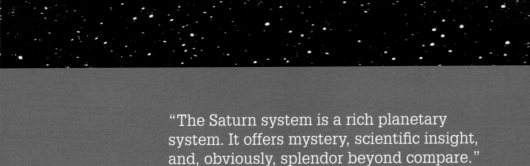

"The Saturn system is a rich planetary system. It offers mystery, scientific insight, and, obviously, splendor beyond compare."
— Dr. Carolyn Porco

Cassini-Huygens: Mission Timeline

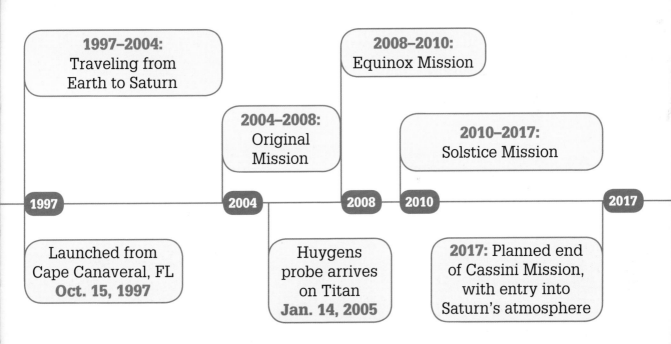

1997–2004:
Traveling from Earth to Saturn

2008–2010:
Equinox Mission

2004–2008:
Original Mission

2010–2017:
Solstice Mission

1997

2004

2008

2010

2017

Launched from Cape Canaveral, FL **Oct. 15, 1997**

Huygens probe arrives on Titan **Jan. 14, 2005**

2017: Planned end of Cassini Mission, with entry into Saturn's atmosphere

What Will Scientists Find Next?

Scientists think learning more about Saturn and its moons will help them learn about Earth's beginnings. The Cassini spacecraft celebrated 10 years of exploring Saturn in 2014. It will continue investigating Saturn's rings and moons until 2017. Cassini will observe the changes in Saturn as the summer season arrives in the northern hemisphere.

When Cassini arrived in 2004, the north pole and its hexagon were dark. The Sun is starting to light up this side of the planet, which will offer scientists a better opportunity to study those features. Cassini will also study Titan's lakes more closely and explore climate changes. It will fly by Enceladus when one of its geysers is shooting out from the moon's surface.

Saturn and its moons are still full of secrets that scientists are working hard to solve. With just a few years left in the mission, they will have to work fast.

Glossary

asteroid (AS-tuh-royd)—a small rocky body that orbits the Sun

astronomy (uh-STRAH-nuh-mee)—the study of stars, planets, and space

atmosphere (AT-muhss-fihr)—the mixture of gases that surrounds a planet or moon

comet (KAH-mit)—a rock that goes around the Sun in a long, slow path; when close to the Sun, it has a long tail of light

diameter (dye-AM-uh-tur)—a straight line through the center of a circle, from one side to another

equator (ee-KWAY-tuhr)—an imaginary line around the middle of a planet that is an equal distance from its north and south poles

erode (ee-ROHD)—to wear down

geyser (GYE-zur)—an underground spring that shoots water, steam, or other material into the air

gravity (GRAV-uh-tee)—the force that pulls things down or to the center of a planet and keeps them from floating away into space

hemisphere (HEM-uhss-fihr)—one half of a sphere, especially of a planet

magnetic field (mag-NEH-tik)—an area of magnetic force around a large object like a planet

methane (METH-ane)—a colorless, odorless gas that can catch fire

mythology (mi-THAH-luh-jee)—a group of myths or stories that belong to a culture

orbit (OR-bit)—the invisible path followed by an object circling a planet, the Sun, etc.

probe (PROHB)—a tool or device used to explore or examine something, as in a space probe

sphere (SFIHR)—a solid shape like a basketball or globe, with all points of the shape the same distance from the center of the shape

vapor (VAY-pur)—particles of moisture in the air

Read More

Lawrence, Ellen. *Saturn: The Ringed Wonder.* New York: Ruby Tuesday Books Ltd., 2013.

Nardo, Don. *Destined for Space: Our Story of Exploration.* Mankato, Minn: Capstone Press, 2012.

Squire, Ann O. *Planet Saturn.* New York: Children's Press, 2014.

Internet Sites

FactHound offers a safe, fun way to find Internet sites related to this book. All of the sites on FactHound have been researched by our staff.

Here's all you do:

Visit www.*facthound.com*

Type in this code: 9781491458686

FactHound will fetch the best sites for you!

 Check out projects, games and lots more at
www.capstonekids.com

Critical Thinking Using the Common Core

1. Read the text on pages 8 and 9. How did each astronomer advance our knowledge of Saturn's rings in the 1600s? (Key Ideas and Details)

2. Read the text on page 24 and look at the image on page 25. How did scientists discover water on Enceladus? Why is that discovery important? (Integration of Knowledge and Ideas)

Index

ancient cultures, 6
atmosphere, 10, 13, 14, 22

bands, 13–14

Cassini Division, 9, 17
Cassini-Huygens, spacecraft, 4, 19–28
Cassini, Jean-Dominique, 9, 19
colors, 4, 13

Earth, 10, 12, 14, 16, 22
Enceladus, 24, 28
equator, 12, 16

Galileo, 8–9
gases, 10
geysers, 24, 28
gravity, 10, 16
Great White Spots, 14

hexagon, 14, 28
Huygens, Christian, 9, 19
Huygens probe, 20, 22–23

ice, 10, 16
interior, 10–13

life, 24

methane, 22
moons, 4, 5, 9, 16, 18–26, 28
mythology, 6, 6–7

North Pole, 14, 28

oceans, 14, 21, 24
orbits, 16–17, 20, 21

Pioneer 11, 18
Porco, Carolyn, 26–27

rings, 4, 5, 6, 8–9, 16–19, 28

seasons, 22, 28
solar system, 4, 16, 20
spokes, 18
storms, 14, 19
Sun, 5, 12, 21, 28

telescopes, 6, 8–9, 26
temperatures, 12, 14, 20
Titan, 9, 20–23, 28

Voyagers, 18–19, 26

water, 10, 24
weather, 12–14